THE OFFICIAL
Celtic
ANNUAL
2002

Written by
Douglas Russell

A Grange Publication

© 2001. Published by Grange Communications Ltd., Edinburgh, under licence from Celtic Football Club. Printed in the EU.

ISBN 1-902704-12-6

£5.99

treble winners

contents

A season in the sun

A look back at Season 2000/01 and how Martin O'Neill's Celtic side brought the glory days back to Paradise with a magnificent 'treble' of Scottish League Championship, Scottish Cup and League Cup.

JULY 2000

The new manager is given an outstanding welcome at Celtic Park as the 'Bhoys' entertain crack French outfit Bordeaux in a pre-season friendly. Although down to ten men, the visitors record an impressive 4-2 victory. New signings, Belgian Joos Valgaeren and Englishman Chris Sutton, take their place in the starting line-up for the opening game of the league campaign against Dundee United at Tannadice. Henrik Larsson scores the opener (surprise, surprise!) before Sutton settles it with another and Celts claim all three points in a 2-1 triumph. An excellent start in high summer and the race has now begun.

AUGUST 2000

The month begins with an edgy 1-0 defeat of Motherwell in the east end of the city (Stilian Petrov scored and both Jackie McNamara and Chris Sutton were dismissed) before UEFA Cup duty 'away' to Jeunesse Esch and a comfortable 4-0 scoreline, with goals from Larsson, Petta and a 'double' from Lubo Moravcik. Back in Glasgow three days later, a hopeful Kilmarnock are the visitors but they return to Ayrshire 'pointless', having lost 2-1.

Henrik and Tommy Johnson (replacing the suspended Sutton) settle the matter. A potentially hazardous trip to the capital's Gorgie Road is next on the agenda, with many neutrals suggesting a possible loss of points. In the event, Celtic are quite superb on the day and Hearts lose out by four goals to two, with Sutton's 'double' the deciding factor. The visit of EUFA Cup opponents Jeunesse is obviously a mere formality after the first leg but, credit to Celtic, they put on a show for over 40,000 fans and add another seven, thus recording an aggregate of 11-0. Three days later, the reigning Champions came calling for the first time that season . . . but the 'Bhoys' were more than ready! In a quite amazing game, Celtic were truly magnificent and destroyed their Ibrox opponents 6-2 with goals from Sutton (2), Petrov, Lambert and Larsson (2). Even at this early stage, many fans were already suggesting the League Title scenario as a very real possibility. In August's games, the team had notted an astonishing 24 times and maintained their 100% record.

SEPTEMBER 2000

The defence of the CIS Insurance Cup began with a comfortable 4-0 win over First Division Raith Rovers, with Tommy Johnson claiming a 'double' and Alan

Thompson netting on his Celtic debut. Uniquely, for the first time in the club's long and illustrious history, all the scorers that night were English, with Chris Sutton completing the trio. The month's 'double' king, however, was Henrik Larsson who netted twice in three consecutive games against Hibernian (3-0, 9.9.2000), HJK Helsinki (2-0, UEFA Cup, 14.9.2000) and Dunfermline in Fife (2-1, 18.9.2000). Stilian Petrov's winner (and only goal of the game) when Ivano Bonetti's Dundee visited from the 'City of Discovery' the following week ensured that Celtic continued to lead from the front in the championship race. Although the team's 100% record in all competitions was halted in Finland during UEFA Cup duty (1-2, 28.9.2000), the 'Bhoys' still progressed to the next stage of this European competition on a 3-2 aggregate score, thanks to a Chris Sutton strike right at the end of extra-time. There was, however, sad news for the club and its fans when midfielder Morten Wieghorst was diagnosed with Guillan-Barre Syndrome after falling ill on the journey back from Scandinavia.

OCTOBER 2000

Although two league points were dropped on a trip to Pittodrie at the beginning of the month (1-1, 1.10.2000), Henrik's valuable, headed equaliser in this finely balanced game with Aberdeen eventually cancelled out Robbie Winters' first-half lead. Newly-promoted St. Mirren appeared in front of their biggest crowd for many a long year two weeks later at Celtic Park (60,002) but, nevertheless, returned to Paisley empty-handed after losing 2-0 and witnessing goals from the deadly duo of Sutton and Larsson. 'Bargain of the Decade' Didier Agathe made his debut after being listed as substitute two weeks earlier in Finland.

Three days later, the location had switched from Glasgow to Perth but the scoreline remained the same with St. Johnstone the 2-0 victims. On this occasion, however, Joos Valgaeren was Henrik's partner in crime. Next it was the turn of Dundee United who, despite putting up a spirited performance, headed back to Tannadice with only memories of a 2-1 loss. The sensational Swede had now scored in four consecutive games for the club. The month ended with two drawn matches, home and abroad. Celtic travelled to Bordeaux in the UEFA Cup (1-1, 26.10.2000) and were rather unlucky not to win, having created most of the real chances during the ninety minutes. Larson's penalty conversion, however, secured a valuable 'away' goal prior to the Glasgow return. Barely 72 hours after the French encounter, Celts lined up at Fir Park to face Motherwell on league business in what proved to be a superb advert for Scottish Football (3-3, 29.10.2000). During October, 'keeper Robert Douglas arrived from Dundee, choosing the green as opposed to the blue of Rangers.

NOVEMBER 2000

It's back to CIS Insurance Cup business on the first of the month when the 'Bhoys' travel east to Tynecastle to face Hearts, with youngsters Healy, Smith and Crainey claiming a first-team start. All three were obviously ready - they each scored in the 5-2 triumph! A difficult 'away' fixture to Kilmarnock secured maximum points (1-0, 5.11.2000) before Bordeaux arrived in Scotland to continue the European joust. However, in a game that Celtic looked to be controlling initially, it was the Gallic visitors who finally took all the honours and progressed in the tournament courtesy of Lilian Laslandes' extra-time winner and 2-1 result. If nothing else, at least Scottish honours now became the only priority. As if to prove the point, Celts banged in ten goals in their next two league outings, with St. Johnstone (4-1, 12.11.2000) and Hearts (6-1, 18.11.2000) the chosen lambs to the slaughter. Lubo Moravcik was well to the fore with goals in both games but Larsson did even better and netted 'doubles' during each of the regulation ninety minutes. Although the month ended on a low due to a 5-1 reversal at Ibrox in the second 'Old Firm' encounter of the season, Celtic were still twelve points ahead of the current champions. A no-scoring draw at Easter Road against high-flying Hibernian three days later (29.11.2000) was enough to suggest that any defeat would, indeed, be a rare occurrence. On a far sadder note, it was announced that Alan Stubbs was once again battling cancer.

SEASON 2000/01 LEAGUE CHAMPIONSHIP QUIZ

1. Who scored Celtic's opening goals of the campaign 'away' to Dundee United in late July 2000?

2. Henrik Larsson netted the winner (and only goal of the game) in Celtic's first 'home' league game of the season. True or false?

3. Name the three teams who were all 'hit for six' at Celtic Park prior to the winter closedown.

4. Who scored consecutive 'doubles' against Dundee United and Kilmarnock in late December and early January respectively?

5. What was the official attendance when Celtic won the Championship on 7 April 2001?

6. Johan Mjallby's first goal of the campaign was in which 'away' game?

7. Robert Douglas made his debut in which league encounter?

8. In the first three league games with Hearts, the 'Bhoys' netted 12 times. True or false?

9. Who were the opponents when Neil Lennon scored his first Celtic goal?

10. Celtic have now won the Scottish League Championship how many times?

7

Answers on page 64.

DECEMBER 2000

It's more like business as usual for this Celtic side at the beginning of the month when Dunfermline are despatched back to the Kingdom of Fife pointless (3-1, 2.12.2000) before the team (including debutant Neil Lennon, just arrived from Leicester where he was O'Neill's on-field lieutenant previously) travelled to Dens Park and a meeting with the impressive Dundee squad.

In the closest of encounters, Didier Agathe's last-gasp, injury-time winner secured full points. By winning this most crucial game (2-1, 10.12.2000), the 'Hoops' were now being spoken about in many quarters as champions-elect. The following week, as if to emphasise the point, victims Aberdeen were well and truly mugged 6-0 in the east end of Glasgow. Not only did 'new-bhoy' Ramon Vega (from Tottenham Hotspur) claim a 'double' in this his first outing for the club but Henrik Larsson netted his first 'hat-trick' of the campaign. Celtic substitute Jamie Smith, who appeared in place of Agathe, was the other scorer in the game.

With Christmas Day celebrations sandwiched between two 'away' outings to St. Mirren and Dundee United, the festive period was in full swing by the time Celtic had collected all six points on the back of 2-0 (23.12.2000) and 4-0 (26.12.2000) victories respectively, with the Boxing Day quartet at Tannadice being particularly impressive. The side had netted seventeen times with the loss of only two goals in the five fixtures that month. Championship material, indeed!

JANUARY 2001

Only one game now remained before the winter shutdown of the Scottish Premier League - Kilmarnock at Celtic Park on 2 January. At the end of this ninety minutes and having suffered the same 6-0 fate as Aberdeen some two weeks earlier, the Ayrshire club no doubt felt that the enforced break was a welcome relief! Larsson was, once again, quite magnificent, scoring four times during the regulation period and, thus, bringing his tally to nine goals in just four games. The other good news, to gladden the hearts of all Celtic fans, was that Paul Lambert, missing since early November with an ankle injury, would soon return.

Following a short break and subsequent training camp in the sun of Florida, the team returned to active Scottish Cup duty (28.1.2001) in the rather cooler surroundings of Stranraer's Stair Park. With defender Joos Valgaeren netting for the fourth time that season (and Lambert, fit again, on the bench) a comfortable 4-1 win was achieved and progress to the next round assured.

TEAM CELTIC QUIZ
TEAM CELTIC QUIZ
TEAM CELTIC QUIZ

1. Name the player who scored twice on his Celtic debut back in December 2000. Who were Celtic's visitors that day?

2. Considered the bargain of the decade by most football observers, how much did Celtic pay Hibernian for Didier Agathe?

3. Chris Sutton's first league goal for the 'Bhoys' was scored where and when?

4. Who scored the only goal of the game when Rangers came calling in February 2001?

5. After captain Tom Boyd, who is Celtic's longest-serving first team player?

6. Who came on as substitute in late February to score the winning goal against Motherwell at Celtic Park?

7. In which game did Henrik Larsson break Charlie Nicholas' post war goal-scoring record?

8. Name the player who scored crucial early season 'home' winners against both Motherwell and Dundee?

9. Who preferred Celtic Park to Ibrox in the autumn of 2000?

10. Whose name was on the championship securing goal v. St. Mirren in early April?

Answers on page 64.

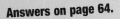

9

FEBRUARY 2001

At the start of the month, the super Swede's third 'hat-trick' of the campaign breaks more than just one heart at Tynecastle Stadium (3-0, 4.2.2001). Considering the facts and figures, this is hardly surprising - the Edinburgh club had now conceded an astonishing eighteen goals to Celts in just three league encounters and one CIS Insurance Cup game! Then, in two games against Rangers in the space of only four days, the club recorded their first back-to-back 'Old Firm' victories since Season 1987/88.

A bruising 3-1 win in the Semi-Final of the CIS Cup at Hampden (goals from Larsson and Sutton in a game that ended with only nineteen players on the park) was followed, thankfully, by a more even-tempered league game at Celtic Park, in which Alan Thompson's solitary strike was enough to claim all three points (1-0, 11.2.2001). Few would dispute that Rangers' championship challenge was now at an end and the trophy would soon be adorned with a different set of colours. Next up was the Forth Road Bridge trip to Dunfermline (on Scottish Cup duty) and an engrossing 2-2 draw (17.2.2001) before two 'home' league games in a row against Motherwell and Hibernian. Once again, the Fir Park outfit provide more than adequate opposition and it takes substitute Lubo Moravcik's priceless goal to win the game (1-0, 21.2.2001). Although Hibernian return with a share of the spoils to Easter Road at the end of that week, Johan Mjallby's goal had preserved Celtic's remarkable, unbeaten home league run (1-1, 25.2.2001) and taken the 'Bhoys' even closer to Scottish Football's Holy Grail.

MARCH 2001

The 'Fifers' of Dunfermline are called upon for the second time in just over two weeks but this time the champions-elect make no mistake and net three without reply - Larsson, Lennon and Petrov are the scorers. The Scottish Cup replay between the same teams at Celtic Park three days later is just as emphatic but this time Larsson and Vega both claim 'doubles' (4-1, 7.3.2001). Hearts are quarter-final opponents in the same competition later that week, with a solitary strike by the 'Super Swede' enough to ensure progress to the semi-final and Dundee United at Hampden. McDiarmid Park is rarely an easy venue but the high-flying 'Bhoys' are more than equal to the task and return home with all three league points in the bag, thanks to goals from Tommy Johnson and Henrik (2-1, 14.3.2001). The championship dream was now close to becoming reality. The season's first silverware arrives in the east end of Glasgow following a comprehensive defeat of Kilmarnock in the CIS Insurance Cup Final (3-0, 18.3.2001). Larsson was simply out of this world and his three goals ensured that Celtic retained this trophy for (at least!) another year.

APRIL 2001

Didier Agathe's winner in the granite city clash with Aberdeen (1-0, 1.4.2001) is followed three days later with another close encounter when Bonetti's ten-man Dundee almost take a point back to Tayside (2-1, 4.4.2001). However, makeshift striker Johan Mjallby's late winner (with just eight minutes remaining) is enough and ensures that only three more points are required before the celebrations can begin in earnest. On 7th April 2001, relegation candidates St. Mirren make the short journey along the

M8 to the Parkhead district of Glasgow probably realising that destiny and the fates are against them! With some 38 minutes on the clock, Tommy Johnson secured his place in the history books by scoring the goal that, by late afternoon, would have 'championship' written all over it. A week later, it was the 'small' matter of a Scottish Cup Semi-Final with Dundee United at Hampden. Henrik netted twice, with Jackie McNamara claiming the other.

At 8.06pm on 22nd April, after the 1-0 victory over Hearts, club captain Tom Boyd held aloft the Bank of Scotland SPL Trophy in front of a delirious crowd of more than 59,000 at Celtic Park. Celebrations were obviously in order and, barely seven days on, would still be heard in the Govan area of the city . . . before, during and after the last 'Old Firm' game of the season! Lubo Moravcik's two goals helped ensure a comprehensive 3-0 Ibrox defeat of Rangers, the first time a Celtic team had triumphed at this venue since August 1994 when both John Collins and Paul McStay netted in a 2-0 victory. The icing on the cake was surely the 'Bhoys' third by Larsson right at the end. Not only was this the striker's 50th goal of the season but it also ensured the club's finest hour in this part of Glasgow for some 30 years. That evening, at the SPFA 'Player of the Year' Dinner, not only did Henrik Larsson win the main award from his fellow professionals but Stilian Petrov was also honoured in the 'Young Player' category.

MAY 2001

As the league campaign drew to a close, there was more than just passing interest in the game against Hibs at Easter Road as the two teams were due to contest the Scottish Cup Final later that month. On a glorious sunny afternoon in the capital, Celts were far too strong for their green counterparts and won with surprising ease (5-2, 6.5.2001). However, the day's obvious delight, for all football supporters regardless of allegiance, was the return of Alan Stubbs to premiership action after his successful battle with cancer. The other scorers in the sun were Jackie McNamara (with a rare 'double'), Henrik and Lubo Moravcik. Although the two final league games of the season against Dundee and Kilmarnock were both lost 2-0 and 1-0 respectively, by far the most important fixture that month was, obviously, the Scottish Cup Final and the very real possibility of a domestic 'treble'. On 26 May at the national stadium, Martin O'Neill's side became the first Celtic team to achieve this feat in thirty-two years when Hibernian were eventually outclassed 3-0. Substitute Jackie McNamara (replacing the injured Lubo Moravcik) claimed number one in the opening period before Larsson netted twice (once from the penalty spot) in the second half. It somehow seemed inevitable that the Swede would score the last goal of the season in addition to claiming the first at Tannadice back in July 2000.

Celtic had travelled a long road since that first league game with Dundee United. In many ways, the journey was just beginning!

legends and heroes

Few Celtic fans have forgotten the veteran Slovak's stunning performance (shortly after arriving in Scotland for that amazingly low fee of just £300,000!) when Rangers were crushed 5-1 in late November 1998. As well as scoring two quite magnificent goals, Lubo was an outfield revelation that day, his almost dream-like movement leaving the baffled, blue rearguard with absolutely no idea of how to contain him. The reigning league champions had been put to the sword, suffering their worst defeat in this part of the city for many a long year.

Fast forward to Govan at the end of April 2001 (and the final 'Old Firm' encounter of the season) and the little man had taken centre stage once again, capturing the headlines as his team won at Ibrox. His superb 'double' strike ensured not only Celtic's first victory at this ground since Season 1994/95 but also a fourth derby triumph for the first time since 1983. Prior to this encounter, Moravcik had already netted ten times for the 'Bhoys' with, probably, his most important goal coming in the February game with Motherwell, after taking the field as substitute and claiming the all-important winner (1-0, 21.2.01). In November, he scored four times in consecutive games against Hearts (CIS Cup), Bordeaux (UEFA Cup) and both St. Johnstone and Hearts (again) in the Premier League. The news that the thirty-five year old was remaining at the club for Season 2001/02 meant that the Slovak would have the opportunity to play in the Champions' League tournament with Celtic. One thing's for sure, Lubo Moravcik will certainly not look out of place in the company of Europe's finest. Why? Because, quite simply, he's one of them!

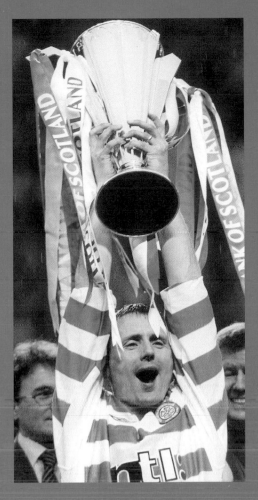

Tom Boyd has now played for a total of eight different bosses at the club - Liam Brady, Lou Macari, Tommy Burns, Wim Jansen, Jo Venglos, John Barnes, Kenny Dalglish and O'Neill himself. For his testimonial game in May 2001, the leading lights of the English Premiership, Manchester United no less, travelled to Glasgow to contest the NTL Champions Challenge Trophy, thus ensuring a 'Battle of Britain' finale to the season.

Prior to this friendly game, Celtic were actually unbeaten in five testimonials with the English giants when, on different occasions, Mark Hughes, Brian McClair, Bryan Robson, Roy Aitken and Paul McStay had all been honoured.

At international level, period 2000/01 was also of supreme importance to the player as, at the ripe old age of thirty-six years, he had won cap number 70 for his country when Scotland met San Marino in a World Cup qualifying game. Few players of the modern era have given so much commitment to both club and country as Tom Boyd of Celtic and Scotland.

Club captain Tom Boyd (Celtic's longest-serving player) proudly held aloft the Championship Trophy back in Season 1997/98, six years after arriving at the club from Chelsea. Some three years later in April 2001, as over 60,000 adoring fans voiced their approval, he repeated the defiant gesture of celebration once again as Celts claimed the title for the 37th time in their history. This time, however, the winning margin between them and Rangers was, shall we say, slightly bigger! Reliable as ever in defence, the Scot had an outstanding season as the 'Bhoys' fired on all cylinders in their pursuit of a glorious domestic treble. With the arrival of Martin O'Neill last season,

It is fair to say that winger Bobby Petta did not enjoy the best of times (or even the best of press) in a Celtic jersey during Season 1999/2000, the Dutchman's first with the Glasgow giants. Let's just say that, the following season, after the 'Old Firm' demolition of Rangers at the beginning of August 2000, more than a few people had dramatically changed their opinion of the player! His 'Man of the Match' performance that day, as he taunted the Ibrox rearguard, was a joy for all Celtic fans to behold. The fact that fellow countryman Fernando Ricksen (his opposite number at the beginning of this particular game) was substituted after just 21 of the most torrid minutes really says it all! A more than interested onlooker that day in the sun was Dutch national team manager Louis Van Gaal, who was no doubt as impressed as everybody else.

Although obviously a supplier of chances rather than a finisher, Bobby actually scored in his first start of the season when Jeunesse Esch visited Glasgow on UEFA Cup duty. Sadly, a persistent groin injury meant that Bobby missed the latter part of the campaign, having been an ever-present in the team from mid October through to the end of January. He did, however, regain fitness in time to make an appearance for Tom Boyd's testimonial game against Manchester United. Having more than played his part in the past season's tremendous success, the future is looking decidedly bright for the entertainer who has already become something of a cult hero with the Celtic legions. Despite never appearing for his country at senior level, Bobby was a regular with both the under-16 and under-18 sides. Many are now suggesting that full international recognition is just around the corner.

Although, understandably, it was that other 'Super Swede' who claimed the 'Player of the Year' title last season, in the eyes of most supporters, Johan Mjallby's contribution to the Celtic cause was no less significant. Maybe his goal tally was not quite as impressive during that fabulous period (he scored four prior to the 'Bhoys' securing the title) but one in particular was of supreme importance. Back in early April, with the Championship still just over the horizon, it looked as if ten-man Dundee would return to Tayside with a precious point following their league game at Celtic Park. With only eight minutes of play remaining, makeshift striker Johan netted the winner (from Alan Thomson's corner) and the scene was set for the very real possibility of a title party three days later. Strangely enough, the giant defender did not start a league game last year until O'Neill's team travelled to Dunfermline in mid September. After that, however, he was virtually an ever-present throughout the long campaign with a series of almost faultless performances in the heart of the Celtic rearguard. Week after week, it seemed as if his penalty box was a 'no go' area for opposition forwards! It should also be noted that when the side were well beaten at Ibrox in late November, the score was still close (at just 1-0 in Rangers' favour) when Mjallby retired injured at half-time. One wonders what the final outcome might have been if he had been able to play the whole ninety minutes. It goes without saying that his intimidating presence is also highly valued by the Swedish national side.

member Jackie McNamara. With manager Martin O'Neill also commenting on the importance of the young Bulgarian throughout the campaign, the accolades continued.

The powerhouse midfielder made 33 starts for the 'Hoops' last year before suffering that horrendous broken ankle in the game with St. Johnstone at McDiarmid Park in the middle of March. His tally of eight goals, from those pre-injury appearances, included three whose category could only be classed as of the 'highly significant' variety! When Motherwell and Dundee came calling in search of precious league points in August and September respectively, both games were decided by a single strike (1-0, 5.8.00 and 1-0, 23.9.00). In each case, Stilian Petrov was the scorer. Sandwiched between the above two ninety minutes was the 6-2 summer annihilation of Rangers. Although his early goal that sun-filled day (with just eight minutes on the clock) was, obviously, not the winner, in many ways it was just as important, ensuring Celts a two goal cushion and really sealing the champions' fate, even at such an early stage of the game.

With European football in place for Season 2001/02, the player hopes to be fit for a return to first-team action before Christmas 2001.

Hopefully, as you're reading this, Stilian will be wearing his beloved green and white colours once again.

Quite rightly voted Scotland's 'Young Player of the Year' for Season 2000/01 by his fellow professionals, Stilian Petrov became the first overseas footballer to win this prestigious honour, following in the footsteps of other Celtic greats such as Charlie Nicholas and Paul McStay as well as current team

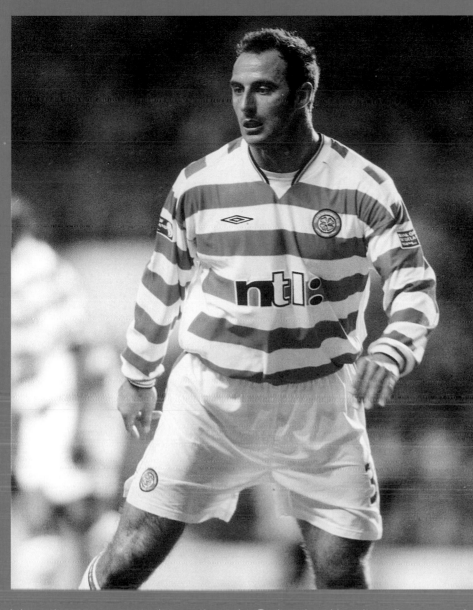

More than one neutral questioned the wisdom of bringing Tottenham Hotspur's Ramon Vega from the south of London to the east end of Glasgow in late 2000 - but it proved to be yet another masterstroke by manager Martin O'Neill in a season when it seemed he definitely had the Midas touch. On his Celtic debut (as Aberdeen were crushed 6-0 in mid December), the powerful Swiss defender not only scored twice but also gave the impression that he had been an integral part of the Celtic set-up for some considerable time, such was his overall contribution on the park that day. We all know that Santa does not originate from Switzerland but it really seemed as if Christmas had arrived just a little early in this part of Glasgow's fair city!

From then on, following his auspicious debut for the 'Hoops', this most cultured of players (and business graduate) never missed a game in the crucial period leading up to the Championship celebrations at Paradise in early April. There was even something of a repeat performance when another 'double' was claimed on the road to Hampden (and a May date with Hibernian) as Dunfermline were beaten 4-1 in the Scottish Cup replay the month before.

ROBERT DOUGLAS

From a neutral point of view, many fans and pundits view Robert Douglas as a future 'No.1' in Craig Brown's international squad. Praise indeed for the young Scottish 'keeper who arrived in Glasgow from Dundee in the winter of 2000, having decided to join Celtic instead of accepting signing-on terms from Rangers. His first-team debut was in the 4-1 'home' victory over St. Johnstone on 12th November. Apart from the CIS Cup games (in which he was 'cup-tied' after appearing in that year's competition with his former club), Douglas was an ever-present in the Celtic starting line up right up to early April's Championship Day celebrations in the east end of the city. In those twenty-three appearances, he recorded a total of thirteen clean sheets. Three weeks later, another 'shut-out' (this time at Ibrox in the final 'Old Firm' league encounter of the season) went a long way to erase any lingering memories of his last visit to Govan with Celtic.

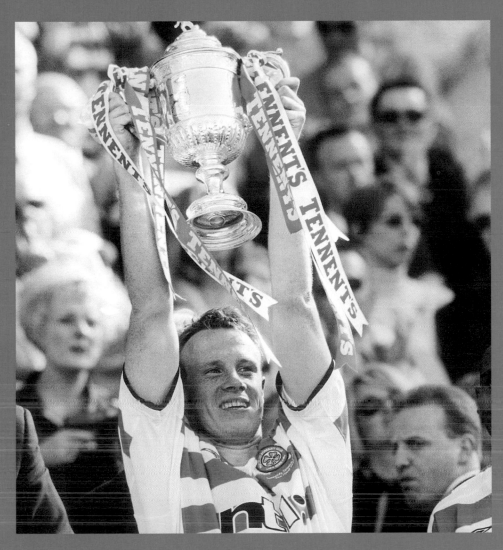

Belgian central defender Joos Valgaeren arrived at Celtic Park following three extremely impressive outings for his country during EURO 2000. Right from the start, it was obvious that Martin O'Neill's purchase was a player of the highest calibre and would have few, if indeed any, problems adjusting to the different style of the Scottish club game. In fact, such was his contribution to the Celtic cause throughout Season 2000/01, many supporters were suggesting 'Defender of the Year' recognition - if such an award category existed!

The big man (who had also interested Leeds United in the summer of 2000) made his debut in green alongside that other newcomer, Chris Sutton, when the 'Bhoys' travelled to Dundee on the very first day of last year's campaign. It was not until mid October that the stopper claimed his own first goal for Celtic - 'away' to St. Johnstone in the 2-0 triumph. The big defender would also strike in the league games with Motherwell (3-3, 29.10.2000) and Hearts (6-1, 18.11.2000) on the road to receiving that Premier Championship Medal he so richly deserved as a stalwart of the Celtic defence.

Prior to reaching these shores, Joos was the proud owner of a Dutch Cup medal (his only senior honour), won with Roda in Season 1999/2000. However, the suspicion remains that an abundance of silverware will be in his possession by the time he eventually leaves our country for good.

It took nearly £6 million to secure the services of Martin O'Neill's midfield lieutenant from English Premiership outfit Leicester City in December 2000. After seeing him play, however (initially filling the injured Paul Lambert's role), the Celtic legions felt that not only was Neil Lennon worth the wait but also something of a bargain as well! His first appearance in club green (as opposed to the green of his country) was the tough 'away' fixture when Bonetti's Dundee provided the opposition in early December (2-1, 10.12.2000). Six days later in Glasgow, Neil's Celtic Park debut was in the pre-Christmas 6-0 demolition of luckless Aberdeen. Seasonal goodwill was obviously not in abundance that day in the east end of the city!

Before long, he was giving the impression of having played for Celtic all his days although, in reality, the player had only recently arrived at his spiritual home. More often than not, with Neil now alongside the likes of Thomson, Petrov and Lambert in the middle of the park, the men in green dominated this crucial area of the field of play. A series of regular powerhouse performances were capped with his first goal 'away' to Dunfermline when the Fifers were beaten 3-0 in early March 2001.

The record books show that, prior to lifting the SPL Title, the 'Bhoys' were only beaten once in that long and arduous campaign. Many would suggest that if a certain blond haired player had been available that November afternoon at Ibrox (remember Paul Lambert was still missing unfit at this stage), the outcome might just have been a little different!

The wing-back, who hails from the small island of Reunion, first appeared in Celtic's starting line-up for the match with St. Mirren in October 2000.

From then on, apart from his substitute role against Kilmarnock in early November, Didier began every league game for his new club as the 'Bhoys' swept all before them on the road to championship glory. The player had arrived from Hibernian in September for the small fee of £35,000, having spent five years in France before coming to Scotland (and Kirkcaldy) to sign for Raith Rovers. Alex McLeish then took Agathe to Easter Road for a brief spell (and his first taste of premiership football) before Martin O'Neill arrived on the scene with an offer from the other side of the country. Right from the start, his Celtic performances were, to say the least, electrifying

(he's probably the quickest player in all of Scottish Football) and the fans soon realised that here was a real, genuine talent with quality to spare.

Prior to that wonderful day when the Paisley side were early April visitors, Didier had netted three times for the club, all in 'away' games. Following his vital late winner against Dundee (2-1, 10.12.2000), the player scored another, two weeks later, when St. Mirren were beaten 2-0. The wing-back then claimed what many considered to be his most important strike of the campaign. At the beginning of April, the 'Bhoys' travelled north to Pittodrie for the Sunday evening clash with Aberdeen, knowing that title celebrations would be so much closer if victory could be achieved. That night, the only goal of the game belonged to Didier Agathe.

PAUL LAMBERT

The Scotland midfielder was an ever-present in the Celtic league line-up from the start of the season right through to early November, before injury deprived Celts of one of their most accomplished players. Returning to active duty for the league clash with Hearts at Tynecastle (3-0, 4.2.2001), the European Cup Winner did not miss another SPL game before St. Mirren travelled across the city from Paisley to Parkhead on that famous early April day.

Everybody accepts that the pairing of Lambert and Neil Lennon in Celtic's midfield was an unqualified success last season. Interestingly enough, right up to when the championship was decided, both players had netted just the once whilst wearing the green. Probably Paul's goal was just that bit more celebrated as it came in the demolition derby of late August when Rangers were crushed 6-2! His Celtic contract expires in year 2003, by which time the player will be thirty-three years old. What happens then is obviously open to debate. Suffice to say that, if nothing else, his unique skills will be on view for at least another two seasons. Reason enough to be thankful.

Voted 'Player of the Year' by his fellow professionals for Season 1997/98, Jackie is now (after club captain Tom Boyd) the longest serving member of the current Celtic first-team squad, having arrived at the club from Dunfermline back in October 1995. Several years prior to that (in March 1989), the player's career was in severe jeopardy after he suffered a quite horrendous injury. At a training session with juvenile side Edina Hibs, his right leg was shattered in two places. Although out of action for seven months, McNamara fought hard to regain his fitness and soon signed for the Fife club.

In Season 2000/01, he began the first league game of the campaign ('away' to Dundee United) and then appeared in the starting line-up another twenty three times before being listed as substitute for the spring championship clincher at Celtic Park against St. Mirren. Jackie even managed goals in consecutive games when Motherwell (3-3, 29.10.2000) and Hearts (5-2, 1.11.2000) were league and CIS Cup opponents respectively although, sadly, he missed the final of the latter competition in March due to suspension.

McNamara did, however, appear in the season's other cup final when he replaced the injured Lubo Moravcik during the first half at Hampden on 26th May. Few need reminding that he scored the all important opener that glorious sunny day in Glasgow.

In his early days with Celtic, the player regularly filled the right fullback position whereas, under Martin O'Neill, Jackie has developed into more of a central midfielder. Regardless of his position, when he pulls on the green, he's still a joy to watch!

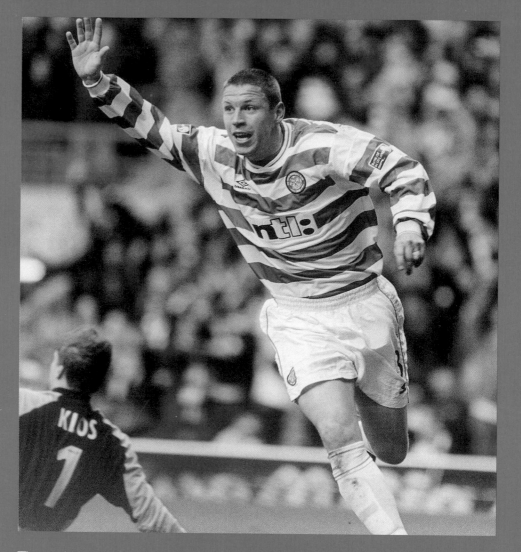

The talented Geordie is another player whose overall contribution to Season 2000/01 cannot be underestimated. An autumnal arrival in Glasgow, from Birmingham, Alan Thompson scored on his Celtic debut when Raith Rovers were beaten 3-0 in the early stages of the CIS Cup back in September 2000. The ex-Aston Villa man also netted against Dundee United (2-1, 21.10.2000) and Kilmarnock (1-0, 5.11.2000) before scoring, by far, his most important strike of the campaign in February 2001. This was, of course, in the 'Old Firm' derby at Celtic Park when his solitary goal, in the 1-0 victory over defending league champions Rangers, ensured three precious points were remaining in the east end of the city.

However, it was his overall play last year (in both attack and defence) that really excited followers of the 'Bhoys' throughout Scotland. Week after week, Thompson gave the very real impression of being that rare individual in today's modern game - a complete midfielder. His work rate was really quite phenomenal! In an attacking sense, more often than not, strikers Chris Sutton or Henrik Larsson were provided with very real scoring chances following typical Thompson deliveries into the opposition penalty area. The words 'deadly accurate' seemed to go hand in hand with either his free kicks or corners.

It really has to be said again - he is a complete midfielder.

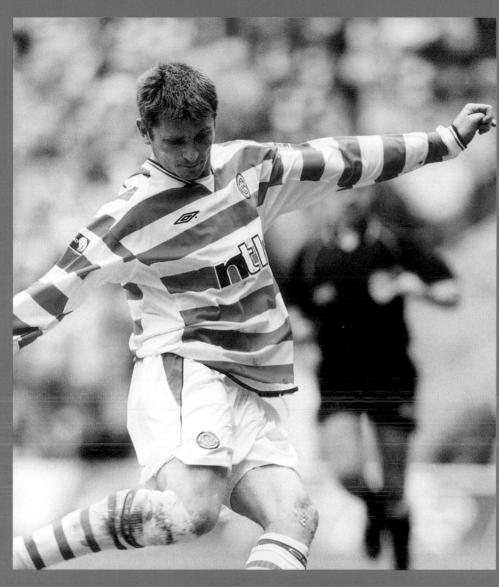

Filling the role of Celtic's third striker (behind, obviously, Henrik Larsson and Chris Sutton), Tommy Johnson entered the history books on 7th April by claiming the goal that finally secured the championship. Interestingly enough, he also scored three days earlier in the close encounter with Dundee at Celtic Park (2-1, 4.4.2001). In both the aforementioned games, the cheerful Geordie was partnering Henrik Larsson up-front due to the unavailability of Chris Sutton, the Swede's normal strike-mate. That famous encounter against St. Mirren had been Johnson's tenth start for the 'Bhoys' last season, with another eleven appearances coming when he took to the field in the role of substitute during a game.

As well as those vital strikes against Dundee and St. Mirren, the player also netted in the matches with Kilmarnock (2-1, 13.8.2000), Raith Rovers (a 'double' in the 4-0 CIS Cup win), Dunfermline (3-1, 2.12.2000) and St. Johnstone (2-1, 14.3.2001). This total of seven goals in ten starts for the club compares favourably with his average the previous season (1999/2000) when the aggregate was ten goals in just eight starting appearances.

Regardless of future events on the transfer front, Tommy Johnson deserves more than just a mention when discussing the fabulous period that was Season 2000/01.

For a striker, former Chelsea man Chris Sutton has a commanding and physical presence second to none in the Scottish Premiership League and proved to be the perfect foil up front for Henrik Larsson last season. Some have suggested that there are striking similarities with Mark Hateley and the successful role that Englishman played in Rangers' team of a few years ago.

Be that as it may, Celtic's six million pound man certainly made his 'mark' right from the start of the campaign, scoring in the opening championship game with Dundee United (2-1, 30.7.2000). The following month, it was a case of consecutive league 'doubles' for the player when Rangers and Hibernian were put to the sword 6-2 and 3-0 respectively. Sutton also claimed twin strikes later on in the season when Dundee United (4-0, 26.12.2000) and Kilmarnock (6-0, 2.1.2001) were comprehensively beaten just before the winter shutdown.

His partnership with Henrik Larsson paid royal dividends throughout the season and watching the two of them complement each other on the field of play was one of the year's true delights for all Celtic-minded people.

Interestingly enough, when Chris missed three league games after the CIS Cup Final (mainly due to a red card that Hampden day), Larsson failed to score in any of those particular games with Aberdeen, Dundee or St. Mirren. But following the Englishman's return for the Scottish Cup semi-final against Dundee United, Henrik netted twice in the 3-1 victory!

The phenomenal goal-scoring feats of Henrik Larsson in Season 2000/01 are discussed in detail elsewhere in this publication (see page 30). Suffice to say that the Swede ('Player of the Year' and surely 'Player of the Decade') is now something of a legend in Paradise.

BANK OF SCOTLAND SCOTTISH PREMIER LEAGUE
SEASON 2000/01

	P	W	D	L	F	A	W	D	L	F	A	GD	PTS
CELTIC	38	17	1	1	49	11	14	3	2	41	18	61	97
RANGERS	38	15	0	4	45	16	11	4	4	31	20	40	82
HIBERNIAN	38	11	6	2	37	15	7	6	6	20	20	22	66
KILMARNOCK	38	7	4	8	20	25	8	5	6	24	28	-9	54
HEARTS	38	11	2	6	36	21	3	8	8	20	29	6	52
DUNDEE	38	4	7	8	25	24	9	1	9	26	25	2	47
ABERDEEN	38	6	6	7	24	24	5	6	8	21		-7	14	45
MOTHERWELL	38	5	4	10	22	27	7	3	9	20	29	-14	43
DUNFERMLINE	38	8	6	5	20	17	3	3	13	14	37	-20	42
ST. JOHNSTONE	38	4	6	9	22	31	5	7	7	18	25	-16	40
DUNDEE UTD.	38	5	6	8	21	28	4	2	13	17	35	-25	35
ST. MIRREN	38	7	3	9	20	25	1	3	15	12	47	-40	30

'IF YOU KNOW THE HISTORY....'

'NINE-IN-A-ROW' QUIZ

1. Which seasons began and ended the legendary '9-in-a-row' sequence?

2. How many goals did Celtic score that year in their 34 league games?

3. In Season 1967/68 Celtic lost only two league games. True or false?

4. Who was top scorer for the team during the above campaign?

5. What was so special about Season 1966/67?

6. Which team finished second in both 1970/71 and 1971/72?

7. An unbeaten run of how many games from February 1973 helped the 'Bhoys' lift the title that year?

8. Celts totalled 57 points in Season 1972/73. What was the Rangers total that campaign?

9. The Scottish Cup was also won in Season 1971/72. Which team did Celtic crush 6-1 in the final?

10. What was Celtic's European Cup record during the '9-in-a-row' sequence?

Answers on page 64.

FIND THE CELT

The names of 10 players who helped bring the Championship back to Celtic Park in Season 2000/01 are hidden in this letter puzzle.

Can you find them?

```
A G E V Q W E R T Y U L B N M L K H G D
P M N B V C X S D L A M B E R T T R E Y
L K J H G F D S A R U Y N L K Z H G F Z
I W E R T D O U G L A S D N O S S R A L
A X E P T U H G I D D Y O B P D F G H K
T B V E X Z D F G H K L P U Y T R E I F
T J H T D X S R T Y W A R A M A N C M G
E O P R K M N Z H G Z V E H T A G A T T
P K M O B G T R D E A W X P Y T D L M I
W E R V F G H K L E N N O N O N P K H W
```

Answers on page 64.

HENRIK LARSSON

SUPER
STRIKER

THE COMPLETE STRIKER

Campaign 2000/2001 was more than just a little special for striker Henrik Larrson, who scored an astonishing 53 goals in all competitions. Not only did he smash Charlie Nicholas' eighteen-year-old post-war record of 48 goals in a season but the player also equalled Brian McClair's 1986/87 tally of 35 Premier League strikes. Few would have considered this extraordinary feat even remotely possible after witnessing the Swede suffer that horrendous leg injury in the French city of Lyon, barely a year-and-a-half earlier, in October 1999. These are the goals that earned Henrik his rightful place in all future history books of the club . . .

LARSSON'S RECORD

Premier League, 30 July 2000
Dundee United (1) Celtic (2)

The first of the many is a left-foot strike curled into the bottom corner of the net.

UEFA Cup, 10 August 2000
Celtic (4) Jeunesse Esch (0)

Henrik's audacious lob leaves the visiting European 'keeper totally helpless.

Premier League, 13 August 2000
Celtic (2) Kilmarnock (1)

Ex-Celt Gordon Marshall is beaten by a low, powerful strike.

Premier League, 19 August 2000
Hearts (2) Celtic (4)

The Swede nets from close in, following up on a long range Paul Lambert effort.

Premier League, 27 August 2000
Celtic (6) Rangers (2)

First 'double' of the campaign comprised a quite stunning lob over the advancing Klos (after Konterman had been skimmed) and a decisive header from Bobby Petta's free-kick. On the day, Rangers were thoroughly and comprehensively thrashed.

Premier League, 9 September 2000
Celtic (3) Hibernian (0)

Another 'double' but this time the combination is a penalty, followed by a headed goal from Lubo Moravcik's superb cross.

UEFA Cup, 14 September 2000
Celtic (2) HJK Helsinki (0)

Claims both goals with a customary, accurate header (courtesy of Jackie McNamara's cross) and a strike from Chris Sutton's pass.

Premier League, 18 September 2000
Dunfermline (1) Celtic (2)

Secures all three points for the 'Bhoys' with, firstly, a converted penalty and then slots home the winner (with just five minutes to go) after good work from Alan Thompson.

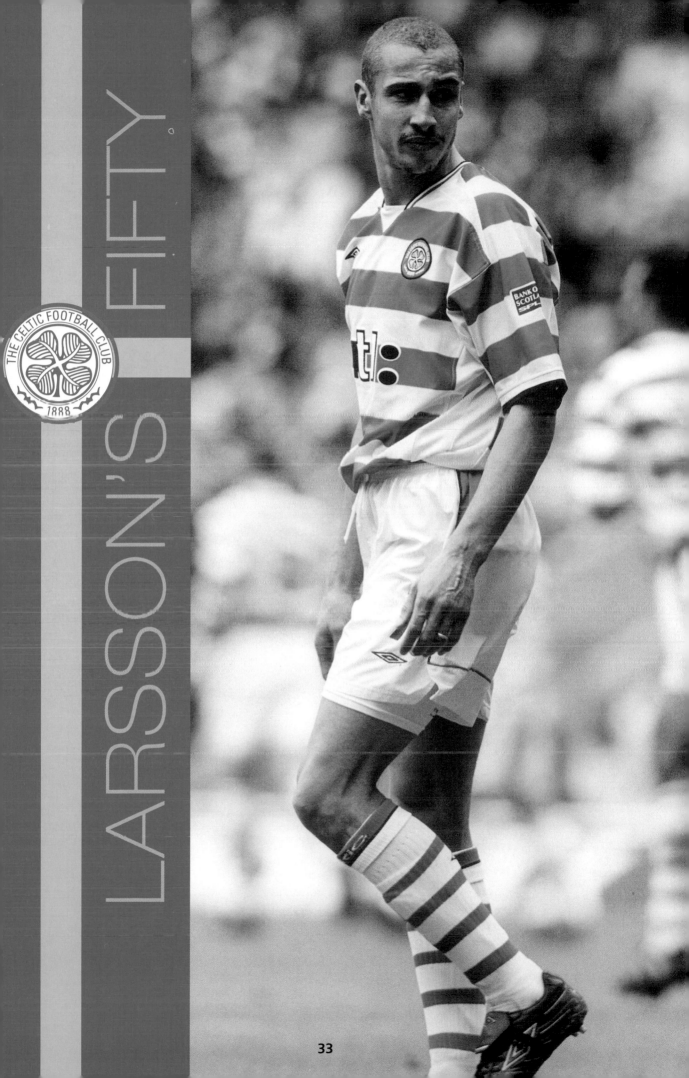

LARSSON'S FIFTY

Premier League, 1 October 2000
Aberdeen (1) Celtic (1)

Minus the famous dreadlocks, Henrik's header from a Lubo cross (with ten minutes remaining) ensures that a point is saved in the granite city.

Premier League, 14 October 2000
Celtic (2) St. Mirren (0)

The Paisley wall of defenders cannot stop his free kick hitting the back of the net.

Premier League, 17 October 2000
St. Johnstone (0) Celtic (2)

Alan Main goes in the opposite direction to Larsson's spot-kick.

Premier League, 21 October 2000
Celtic (2) Dundee United (1)

A rocket header from Stillian Petrov's corner.

UEFA Cup, 26 October 2000
Bordeaux (1) Celtic (1)

After dusting himself down, Henrik duly converts the penalty he has just won.

Premier League, 12 November 2000
Celtic (4) St. Johnstone (1)

An accurate finish, with his right foot, is the first of a 'double' which also includes one of his now-trademark, audacious lobs.

Premier League, 18 November 2000
Celtic (6) Hearts (1)

Second 'double' in the space of a week, beating Niemi from close in (after the Hearts 'keeper had blocked his initial shot) and then calmly netting Tommy Johnson's lay-off.

Premier League, 26 November 2000
Rangers (5) Celtic (1)

A headed equaliser (early in the second half) from Alan Thompson's beautifully flighted corner kick.

Premier League, 2 December 2000
Celtic (3) Dunfermline (1)

Pars 'keeper Ruitenbeek is a Larsson nutmeg victim.

Premier League, 16 December 2000
Celtic (6) Aberdeen (0)

Two strikes, from a Bobby Petta cross and a Tommy Johnson pass, are more than complemented by a thunderous top corner volley and the 'hat-trick' is complete.

Premier League, 23 December 2000
St. Mirren (0) Celtic (2)

Stillian Petrov was the provider and Henrik once again the close range finisher.

Premier League, 26 December 2000
Dundee United (0) Celtic (4)

It's the last game of the year and Larsson is just about to hit goal number 28! His penalty conversion is as clinical as ever.

Premier League, 2 January 2001
Celtic (6) Kilmarnock (0)

Not such a 'Happy New Year' for the Ayrshire club as they are crushed and Henrik claims four more, including a nutmeg on 'keeper Marshall.

Premier League, 4 February 2001
Hearts (0) Celtic (3)

The striker nets all three Celtic goals, starting with a downward header past Niemi and then finishing off crosses from both Alan Thompson and Didier Agathe respectively.

CIS Insurance Cup, 7 February 2001
Celtic (3) Rangers (1)

The tally rises to five in the space of a week with two in this 'Old Firm' cup tie. The first is a lob over Klos (again!) after winning possession from defender Malcolm and the second a penalty, both won and despatched by the Swede.

Scottish Cup, 17 February 2001
Dunfermline (2) Celtic (2)

Another 'double' to keep the 'Treble' dreams alive. Heads home from an Alan Thompson free kick then scores from close in after good work by Chris Sutton.

Premier League, 4 March 2001
Dunfermline (0) Celtic (3)

A magnificent free kick finds the top corner of the net and the Pars suffer yet again at his hands . . . or should that be feet!

Scottish Cup, 7 March 2001
Celtic (4) Dunfermline (1)

Two spot kicks (after the player himself had been fouled in the box on each occasion) complete a rather nice twosome.

Scottish Cup, 11 March 2001
Celtic (1) Hearts (0)

The winner is another magnificent Larsson header, once again courtesy of an Alan Thompson cross.

Premier League, 14 March 2001
St. Johnstone (1) Celtic (2)

A delicate header from (yes!) Alan Thompson's free-kick.

CIS Insurance Cup Final, 18 March 2001
Celtic (3) Kilmarnock (0)

Without a shadow of doubt, this was the final of Henrik Larsson. His trilogy of strikes comprised a superb hook shot (that left Marshall well beaten), a deflected shot (via defender Innes) and a goal of genuine magic when he rounded the 'keeper after bursting through the Kilmarnock defence. The season's first silverware was on its way to the east end of Glasgow.

Scottish Cup Semi-Final, 15 April 2001
Celtic (3) Dundee United (1)

Larsson's brave, flying header from Chris Sutton's penetrating cross was goal number 48 of the season and equalled the post-war Celtic record of Charlie Nicholas. A second-half penalty, both won and converted by our man, ensured that the previous, long-standing record had now gone.

Premier League, 29 April 2001
Rangers (0) Celtic (3)

The half-century and goal number 50 came less than five minutes before the end of the final 'Old Firm' game of the season at Ibrox. Taking Jackie McNamara's pass inside the box, Henrik rounded the Rangers 'keeper, Klos, before slotting home, from the tightest of angles, for a quite superb finish. A marvellous end to the most marvellous of days!

Premier League, 6 May 2001
Hibernian (2) Celtic (5)

Larsson's second-half strike (in this dress rehearsal for the Scottish Cup Final) meant that Brian McClair's record of 35 Premier League goals (in Season 1986/87) had now been equalled as the 'Bhoys cruised to victory with the most convincing capital display. Surprisingly, it was the striker's first-ever goal at Easter Road.

Two minutes into the second period (with Celtic leading 1-0), he claimed the first of a cup final 'double' with a fine left-foot strike from just inside the box, after collecting McNamara's pass. The player's second of the afternoon was a penalty after he had been brought down by defender Gary Smith whilst chasing a Sutton through ball. Fittingly, the Swede, who had scored Celtic's opening goal of the campaign at Tannadice, was also responsible for his side's last.

From late July 2000 to early summer 2001, Henrik Larsson's personal tally was an astonishing 53 goals.

celtic legends
quiz

1. How many League Championships and Scottish Cup triumphs did Celtic achieve under Jock Stein?

2. Name the player who scored a 'hat-trick' in the League Cup Final of 1957, when Rangers were famously beaten 7-1?

3. Who was captain that glorious day?

4. Who netted Celtic's second goal in the European Cup Final of 1967?

5. He made his first-team debut against Aberdeen in January 1982 and would go on to make some 514 league appearances for the club. Name him.

6. The first player from either side to claim a 'hat-trick' in an 'Old Firm' Scottish Cup Final was . . .

7. Such was his early standing in the team, that a common joke of the period suggested that this player paid no income tax as he supported ten dependants in Celtic colours! Name the legend.

8. A hero with both Celtic and Leeds United fans, he was nicknamed the 'Pocket Dynamo' during his time in Glasgow. Name him.

9. Billy McNeill said that "he knows what wearing a Celtic jersey means." Name the great striker.

10. Whose two late goals in the 1988 Scottish Cup Final clinched the Centenary 'double' for the club.

Answers on page 64.

SLAUGHTER IN

CELTIC 6   RANGERS 2

Sutton (1, 90), Petrov (8), Lambert (11), Larsso
Premier League, 27 August 2000

THE SUN

(50, 62)

No doubt, the defending champions arrived in the east end of Glasgow full of confidence. After all, the Ibrox outfit had won the previous season's title by a huge margin of twenty-one points from Celtic and had already netted thirteen goals in the first four games of this new league campaign. With their increased pool of players, they were, understandably, strong favourites to lift the trophy for a third consecutive year. However Celtic, ready and waiting, had other ideas and were about to issue a storm warning to all of Scottish football. A hurricane was on the way . . . even although a sunny Sunday had been forecast for much of the country!

Amazingly, with barely a minute on the clock, Celts were in front. Following Lubo's corner, a mis-cued Larsson effort fell to new 'Bhoy' Chris Sutton who buried the ball from close range past Klos in the Rangers goal. Paradise erupted. Seven minutes later, another superbly-flighted corner from Moravcik was met by the head of Stilian Petrov (who had ghosted into the penalty area) and the German

'keeper was beaten again. Two goals in just eight minutes of play - surely it couldn't get any better? Well, not for another three minutes anyway!

Paul Lambert obviously felt that it was time for a Scot to get in on the scoring act so, after excellent build-up work from Moravcik, the midfielder blasted a powerful right foot shot from some fifteen yards past Klos for Celtic's third, with the stadium clock not even having registered a quarter of an hour. Although the visitors pulled one back (courtesy of

Claudio Reyna) just before half-time, the teams left the field at the interval with the 'Bhoys' well in command. Right at the start of the second period, Henrik Larsson netted his first of the afternoon. And, it must be said, a goal to remember for a very long time. Jonathan Gould's long kick was controlled (and passed!) by the chest of Chris Sutton to his Swedish striking partner. Larsson then skimmed central defender Konterman

before audaciously chipping the advancing Rangers 'keeper from outside the box for one of the truly great 'Old Firm' goals.

The visitors then pulled one back with a Billy Dodds penalty before Henrik made it five (on the 62 minute mark), heading home from Bobby Petta's excellent free-kick. Even at 5-2, Celtic kept pressing and were duly rewarded right at the end when Chris Sutton claimed his second of the day following Stephane Mahe's accurate, low cross into the box. Needless to say, Rangers greeted the sound of the final whistle with more than just a little relief! Although, in terms of the championship race, this amazing victory was still only worth three points, a massive psychological blow had been struck. The road to the SPL title was indeed a long one but Martin O'Neill's side had proved, even at this early stage, that they were ready for the journey ahead. The storm clouds over this part of the city may have passed by late afternoon but the Celtic hurricane would soon return.

Celtic : Gould, Mahe, McNamara, Valgaeren, Stubbs, Lambert, Petta, Petrov, Moravcik, Larsson and Sutton.

ONE DOWN, TWO TO GO!

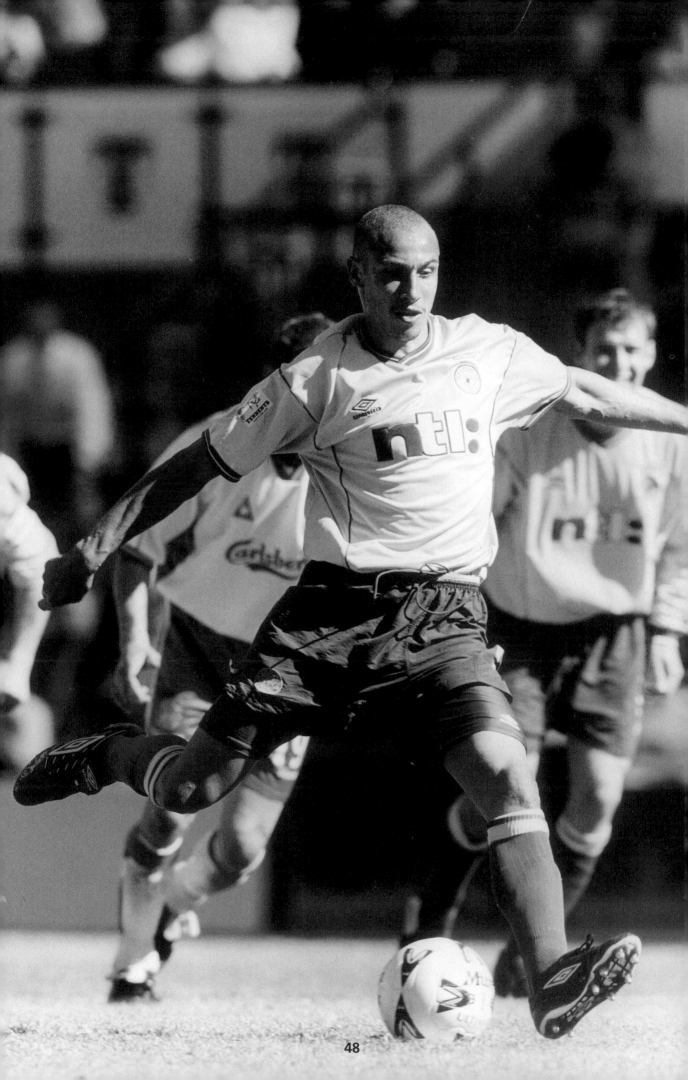

OLD FIRM QUIZ

1. Who scored the Celtic goals when Rangers were crushed 6-2 in late August 2000?

2. What was unique about Chris Sutton's goals during the above game?

3. Celtic were due to play Rangers for the 'Victory In Europe' Cup in May 1945. What happened?

4. Alan Thompson netted when Rangers were beaten 3-1 in the semi-final of the CIS Cup last season. True or false?

5. Prior to lifting the European Cup in May 1967, Celtic met Rangers at Ibrox in the last league game of that season. What was the score?

6. Although established as first-choice 'keeper, Robert Douglas missed the game with Rangers on 7 February 2000. Why?

7. Name the Italian who netted for Celts in the 2-0 Scottish Cup quarter-final victory of March 1997.

8. Whose playing career was ended by an ankle injury sustained against Rangers in the autumn of 1955?

9. His early goal was the beginning of a crushing 4-0 Scottish Cup Final win in 1969. Name the legendary captain of Celtic.

10. What was unusual about Brian McClair's 'hat-trick' in the game with Rangers in the early part of Season 1983/84?

Answers on page 64.

CIS Cup Final

CELTIC 3   KILMARNOCK 0
Larsson (48, 75 and 81)

In years to come, no doubt, this ninety minutes will be remembered as the final of Henrik Larsson. The sensational Swede claimed all three of Celtic's goals, becoming the first player to score a League Cup Final hat-trick since Ally McCoist way back in 1984. It is worth noting that two of his goals came at a stage in the game when the 'Bhoys' had been reduced to ten men following the second-half dismissal of striking partner Chris Sutton. Prior to kick-off, the Glasgow side were certainly hot favourites, not only in the eyes their own fans but also with the majority of neutrals as well. An understandable reaction when you consider the fact that Celtic had powered their way to Hampden, taking the scalps of Raith Rovers (4-0), Hearts (5-2) and, best of all, Rangers (3-1) along the way. As with most of Season 2000/01, it was a rare side that could even dent their pursuit of glory.

After a barren first-half (in terms of scoring), Larsson struck almost immediately after the break. Following Moravcik's cross into the box, Ramon Vega set up a chance from which the striker netted with a hook shot past ex-Celt Gordon Marshall in goal. The Swede's second of the day, with some fifteen minutes remaining, was a deflected shot past the Kilmarnock 'keeper via defender Innes. His third (as the Ayrshire side pushed forward in search of some consolation) was the pick of the bunch, after bursting through and rounding Marshall to finish with some considerable style. Henrik Larsson's day was complete. Celtic had successfully defended the trophy won the previous March when Aberdeen had been their Hampden opponents and victims. Only this time, one year on, Martin O'Neill's side had just secured the first leg of a possible treble. And celebrations for part two of that particular quest were just over the horizon and only a matter of three weeks away.

Celtic : Gould, Valgaeren, Vega, Mjallby, Petta, Lennon, Lambert, Healy, Moravcik, Larsson and Sutton.

Scottish Cup Final

26 May 2001

CELTIC 3 HIBERNIAN 0
McNamara (38), Larsson (47, 80)

Surprisingly, Celtic had not won a domestic 'treble' since the famous 'Lisbon Lions' achieved this impressive feat back in Season 1968/69. Thirty-two years on, Martin O'Neill's side (a true band of brothers) stood on the verge of greatness as they lined up for the final of the Scottish Cup, having already lifted both the Championship and League Cup trophies with style to spare. One final flourish was all that was required for this class of 2001 to join the ranks of those legends from Celtic's illustrious past. However, Hibernian had finished an excellent third in the SPL and, not having won the Scottish Cup since 1902, would be more than just determined opponents. Manager Alex McLeish certainly wasn't bringing his team to Hampden just to make up the numbers! An intriguing game was in prospect.

In fact, the Edinburgh outfit, after surviving a traditional early Celtic onslaught, began to play with no small amount of confidence for the first half-hour. Despite this, however, it was the 'Bhoys' who took the lead when Jackie McNamara (a substitute for the injured Moravcik) steered the ball past 'keeper Colgan after being set up by Didier Agathe in thirty-eight minutes. First blood to the champions. As half-time approached, the Hibernian rearguard were no doubt quite relieved to have, at least, kept Henrik Larsson at bay. That would certainly not be the case in the second period of the game.

Within just two minutes of the restart, and with McNamara involved again but this time as provider, the Swede made his mark with goal number 52 of the season. A powerful left foot shot (as defender Fenwick slipped), from some twelve yards, left Colgan with no chance at all. Then, in the 80th minute, he netted his second of the afternoon - this time from the penalty spot (after a foul by Gary Smith as he chased a Sutton through ball) with a right foot finish. It was all over bar the 'treble yells' from the Celtic masses gathered inside the national stadium!

Martin O'Neill's hard-working team had achieved what many considered to be impossible less than a year ago. It really had been the most magical of seasons.

Celtic : Douglas, Mjallby, Vega, Valgaeren, Agathe, Lambert, Lennon, Thompson, Moravcik, Larsson and Sutton.

SCOTTISH C
2000

IP WINNERS 2001

NNENT'S

OTTISH CUP
WINNERS 2001

OLD BHOY

PREMIER LEAGUE, 29 APRIL 2001

RANGERS 0 CELTIC 3

MORAVCIK (61, 73), LARSSON (86)

Of course, by this stage of the league season, the SPL Trophy was already in pride of place at Celtic Park, adorned in green and white ribbons. Nevertheless, there was still a great deal at stake for both sides prior to this Ibrox showdown and last 'Old Firm' encounter of the 2000/01 period.

The 'Bhoys' had suffered an embarrassing 5-1 reversal on their last visit to Govan (and were obviously out for revenge) whereas Rangers were looking to finish their failed challenge with a morale-boosting victory over the newly-crowned champions and best team in the land. Although the home side had the better of the first half, it was still 0-0 at the interval. Then, half way through the second period, the deadlock was finally broken by a little piece of magic (not for the first time!) from Moravcik, the wizard. Taking a Larsson return pass just outside the penalty area, the Slovak headed for the Rangers goal and finished in style with a low shot past their German 'keeper. That was good but even better was to follow. In 73 minutes, he gathered a Maloney head-flick and made a bee-line towards Klos again, superbly turning Dutch defender Ricksen before scoring his second of the game. And how the Celtic faithful in the Broomloan Road stand celebrated what had been a quite marvellous individual show from the 'Old Bhoy' himself! Not for the first time had Moravcik played a major role in the destruction of Rangers.

As if to ensure that his team-mate didn't grab all the headlines in the following day's papers, Larsson netted number three with just four minutes left to play. This goal created two records. Firstly, it was the Swede's 50th strike of the season and, secondly, it meant that Rangers (by losing 3-0) had suffered their biggest home 'Old Firm' defeat for thirty years. In more ways than one, those avenging angels in green had taken their revenge.

Celtic : Douglas, Mjallby, Vega, Valgaeren, Agathe, Lambert, Lennon, Thompson, Moravcik, Larsson and Johnson.

RANGERS CELTIC

0 - 3

PREMIER LEAG
2000

THE CELTIC FOOTBALL CLUB 1888

BANK

2000 - 2

BANK OF SCOTLAND SPL

IE CHAMPIONS
2001

OF SCOTLAND

01   CHAMPIONS

ANSWERS

SEASON 2000/01 LEAGUE CHAMPIONSHIP QUIZ

1. Henrik Larsson and Chris Sutton. 2. False. It was Stilian Petrov. 3. Rangers, Hearts and Aberdeen.
4. Chris Sutton. 5. 60,440. 6. 3-3 at Motherwell, 29.10.2000. 7. v. St. Johnstone, 12.11.2000.
8. False. It was 13 times! 9. Dunfermline, 4.3.2001. 10. 37.

TEAM CELTIC QUIZ

1. Ramon Vega. Aberdeen. 2. £35,000!!! 3. Tannadice v. Dundee United, 30.7.2000. 4. Alan Thompson.
5. Jackie McNamara. 6. Lubo Moravcik. 7. Scottish Cup Semi-Final, 15.4.2001 v. Dundee United.
8. Stilian Petrov. 9. Robert Douglas when he arrived from Dundee. 10. Tommy Johnson.

NINE-IN-A-ROW QUIZ

1. 1965/66 and 1973/74. 2. 106. 3. False. They lost only one. 4. Bobby Lennox, with 32 goals.
5. Celtic won all Scottish domestic honours plus, of course, the European Cup. 6. Aberdeen.
7. 14. 8. 56 points. 9. Hibernian. 10. They reached the final twice and the semi-final twice.

CELTIC LEGENDS QUIZ

1. 10 League Championships and 8 Scottish Cups. 2. Billy McPhail. 3. Bertie Peacock. 4. Steve Chalmers.
5. Paul McStay. 6. Jimmy Quinn, in 1904. 7. Charlie Tully. 8. Bobby Collins. 9. Bobby Lennox.
10. Frank McAvennie's.

OLD FIRM QUIZ

1. Sutton (2), Petrov, Lambert and Larsson(2). 2. His two strikes were scored in the first and last minutes
of the game. 3. Rangers declined on account of having another cup final the following week.
Celts played Queens Park instead. 4. False. He scored against them four days later in the league.
5. A 2-2 draw. 6. He was 'cup-tied' with Dundee. 7. Paolo Di Canio. 8. Jock Stein. 9. Billy McNeill.
10. He was still a Motherwell player at the time!

WORDSEARCH

```
A G E V Q W E R T Y U L B N M L K H G D
P M N B V C X S D L A M B E R T T R E Y
L K J H G F D S A R U Y N L K Z H G F Z
I W E R T D O U G L A S D N O S S R A L
A X E P T U H G I D D Y O B P D F G H K
T B V E X Z D F G H K L P U Y T R E I F
T J H T D X S R T Y W A R A M A N C M G
E O P R K M N Z H G Z V E H T A G A T T
P K M O B G T R D E A W X P Y T D L M I
W E R V F G H K L E N N O N O N P K H W
```